My FAMILY RECORD

The Rest of the Story

Editor's Note

My Family Record begins with a family tree and page references for your convenience in compiling your loved ones' important moments, memorable stories, and best-loved photographs, within a framework designed for either traditional or nontraditional families.

If this book is intended as a gift for your child or another young family member, there are areas for completion in later years. An heirloom may be created for future family members by "working backwards," recording yourself as grandparent and your parents as great-grandparents, saving room for future in-laws to make handwritten contributions for your mutual grandchildren.

You will notice that in each section there are special spaces for "The rest of the story," provided for those family-specific details so seldom recorded on paper, such as the way your youngest discovered the Easter Bunny, how a favorite uncle really lost his first job, descriptions of your first automobile, or the silliest prank you ever played on an unsuspecting brother or sister. Simply use your imagination for "The rest of the story."

Before you begin, carefully peruse the pages and entry spaces within *My Family Record*. Feel free to photocopy blank pages for additional or extended family members and slip them into an envelope and attach it to the back of the book.

We suggest you invite other relatives, and even current or former in-laws, to help fill in pages from their own perspectives, in their own handwriting. An advantage to this kind of teamwork is that it provides each member with the candor to create a truly personal family record. Just imagine how much more "objective" your sister will be if she records your worst childhood mischief. Just picture the delight future generations will find in a hand-wrought tapestry of memories.

Book concept and text: Robin Crouch
Editorial Assistant: Judy Van Dyke
Design and illustration: Camille Engel
Typography: Mark Foltz

Published by Great American Opportunities, Inc.
2451 Atrium Way
Nashville, TN 37214
1-800-358-0560

ISBN: 0-87197-814-8

Manufactured in the United States of America
First Printing: 1995, 50,000 copies

Family Tree

You
pages 4–5
Sibling
pages 6–7
Sibling
pages 8–9
Mother
pages 12–13
Aunt/Uncle
pages 14–15
Aunt/Uncle
pages 16–17
Father
pages 30–31
Aunt/Uncle
pages 32–33
Aunt/Uncle
pages 34–35
Grandmother
pages18–19
Grandfather
pages 24–25
Great-Grandmother
pages 26–27
Great-Grandfather
pages 28–29
Great-Grandmother
pages 20–21
Great-Grandfather
pages 22–23
Grandmother
pages36–37
Grandfather
pages 42–43
Great-Grandmother
pages 44–45
Great-Grandfather
pages 46–47
Great-Grandmother
pages 38–39
Great-Grandfather
pages 40–41

You

Full name

Date & place of birth

Birth weight length eye color hair color

First crawled at age months First tooth at age months

First walked at age months

Family resemblances

Brothers' & sisters' names & dates of birth

Babyhood personality & antics

First religious ceremony & attendants

Childhood home(s)

Friends & pets of childhood

Relationships with siblings

Funniest moments

Special talents & activities

affix photo here if desired

Childhood mischief

Proudest moments

School performance & dreams

Fads, phases & crazes

Education/occupation/military service

How you remember meeting your husband/wife

Your wedding date, place & your funniest memory

The rest of the story

Your Sibling

Full name

Date & place of birth

Birth weight length eye color hair color

First crawled at age months First tooth at age months

First walked at age months

Family resemblances

Babyhood personality & antics

First religious ceremony & attendants

Childhood home(s)

Friends & pets of childhood

Relationships with siblings

Funniest moments

Special talents & activities

Childhood mischief

affix photo here if desired

Proudest moments

School performance & dreams

Fads, phases & crazes

Education/occupation/military service

How he/she remembers meeting his/her husband/wife

His/Her best memories of courtship

His/Her wedding date, place & his/her funniest memory

The rest of the story

Your Sibling

Full name

Date & place of birth

Birth weight length eye color hair color

First crawled at age months First tooth at age months

First walked at age months

Family resemblances

Babyhood personality & antics

First religious ceremony & attendants

Childhood home(s)

Friends & pets of childhood

Relationships with siblings

Funniest moments

Special talents & activities

Childhood mischief

affix photo here if desired

Proudest moments

School performance & dreams

Fads, phases & crazes

Education/occupation/military service

How he/she remembers meeting his/her husband/wife

His/Her best memories of courtship

His/Her wedding date, place & his/her funniest memory

The rest of the story

Family Photographs

Family Photographs

Your Mother

Full name

Date & place of birth

Birth weight length eye color hair color

Family resemblances

Brothers' & sisters' names & dates of birth

First religious ceremony & attendants

Childhood home(s)

Friends & pets of childhood

Relationships with siblings

Fondest memories

Funniest moments

Special talents & activities

Childhood mischief

affix photo here if desired

Proudest moments

School performance & dreams

Fads, phases & crazes

Education/occupation

How she remembers meeting your father

Her best memories of courtship

Her wedding date, place & her funniest memory

The rest of the story

Your Aunt or Uncle *Your Mother's Sibling*

Full name

Date & place of birth

Birth weight length eye color hair color

Family resemblances

First religious ceremony & attendants

Childhood home(s)

Friends & pets of childhood

Relationships with siblings

Fondest memories

Funniest moments

Special talents & activities

Childhood mischief

Proudest moments

School performance & dreams

affix photo here if desired

Fads, phases & crazes

Education/occupation/military service

How he/she remembers meeting your uncle/aunt

His/Her best memories of courtship

His/Her wedding date, place & his/her funniest memory

Children's names and dates of birth

The rest of the story

Your Aunt or Uncle *Your Mother's Sibling*

Full name

Date & place of birth

Birth weight length eye color hair color

Family resemblances

First religious ceremony & attendants

Childhood home(s)

Friends & pets of childhood

Relationships with siblings

Fondest memories

Funniest moments

Special talents & activities

Childhood mischief

Proudest moments

affix photo here if desired

School performance & dreams

Fads, phases & crazes

Education/occupation/military service

How he/she remembers meeting your uncle/aunt

His/Her best memories of courtship

His/Her wedding date, place & his/her funniest memory

Children's names and dates of birth

The rest of the story

Your Grandmother *Your Mother's Mother*

Full name

Date & place of birth

Birth weight length eye color hair color

Family resemblances

Brothers' & sisters' names & dates of birth

First religious ceremony & attendants

Childhood home(s)

Friends & pets of childhood

Relationships with siblings

Fondest memories

Funniest moments

Special talents & activities

Childhood mischief

Proudest moments

affix photo here if desired

School performance & dreams

Fads, phases & crazes

Education/occupation

How she remembers meeting your grandfather

Her best memories of courtship

Her wedding date, place & her funniest memory

The rest of the story

Your Great-Grandmother *Your Mother's Mother's Mother*

Full name

Date & place of birth

Birth weight length eye color hair color

Family resemblances

Brothers' & sisters' names & dates of birth

First religious ceremony & attendants

Childhood home(s)

Friends & pets of childhood

Relationships with siblings

Fondest memories

Funniest moments

Special talents & activities

Childhood mischief

affix photo here if desired

Proudest moments

School performance & dreams

Fads, phases & crazes

Education/occupation

How she remembers meeting your great-grandfather

Her best memories of courtship

Her wedding date, place & her funniest memory

The rest of the story

Your Great-Grandfather *Your Mother's Mother's Father*

Full name

Date & place of birth

Birth weight length eye color hair color

Family resemblances

Brothers' & sisters' names & dates of birth

First religious ceremony & attendants

Childhood home(s)

Friends & pets of childhood

Relationships with siblings

Fondest memories

Funniest moments

Special talents & activities

Childhood mischief

affix photo here if desired

Proudest moments

School performance & dreams

Fads, phases & crazes

Education/occupation/military service

How he remembers meeting your great-grandmother

His best memories of courtship

His wedding date, place & his funniest memory

The rest of the story

Your Grandfather *Your Mother's Father*

Full name

Date & place of birth

Birth weight length eye color hair color

Family resemblances

Brothers' & sisters' names & dates of birth

First religious ceremony & attendants

Childhood home(s)

Friends & pets of childhood

Relationships with siblings

Fondest memories

Funniest moments

Special talents & activities

Childhood mischief

affix photo here if desired

Proudest moments

School performance & dreams

Fads, phases & crazes

Education/occupation/military service

How he remembers meeting your grandmother

His best memories of courtship

His wedding date, place & his funniest memory

The rest of the story

Your Great-Grandmother *Your Mother's Father's Mother*

Full name

Date & place of birth

Birth weight length eye color hair color

Family resemblances

Brothers' & sisters' names & dates of birth

First religious ceremony & attendants

Childhood home(s)

Friends & pets of childhood

Relationships with siblings

Fondest memories

Funniest moments

Special talents & activities

Childhood mischief

affix photo here if desired

Proudest moments

School performance & dreams

Fads, phases & crazes

Education/occupation

How she remembers meeting your great-grandfather

Her best memories of courtship

Her wedding date, place & her funniest memory

The rest of the story

Your Great-Grandfather *Your Mother's Father's Father*

Full name

Date & place of birth

Birth weight length eye color hair color

Family resemblances

Brothers' & sisters' names & dates of birth

First religious ceremony & attendants

Childhood home(s)

Friends & pets of childhood

Relationships with siblings

Fondest memories

Funniest moments

Special talents & activities

Childhood mischief

affix photo here if desired

Proudest moments

School performance & dreams

Fads, phases & crazes

Education/occupation/military service

How he remembers meeting your great-grandmother

His best memories of courtship

His wedding date, place & his funniest memory

The rest of the story

Your Father

Full name

Date & place of birth

Birth weight length eye color hair color

Family resemblances

Brothers' & sisters' names & dates of birth

First religious ceremony & attendants

Childhood home(s)

Friends & pets of childhood

Relationships with siblings

Fondest memories

Funniest moments

Special talents & activities

Childhood mischief

affix photo here if desired

Proudest moments

School performance & dreams

Fads, phases & crazes

Education/occupation/military service

How he remembers meeting your mother

His best memories of courtship

His wedding date, place & his funniest memory

The rest of the story

Your Aunt or Uncle *Your Father's Sibling*

Full name

Date & place of birth

Birth weight length eye color hair color

Family resemblances

First religious ceremony & attendants

Childhood home(s)

Friends & pets of childhood

Relationships with siblings

Fondest memories

Funniest moments

Special talents & activities

Childhood mischief

Proudest moments

affix photo here if desired

School performance & dreams

Fads, phases & crazes

Education/occupation/military service

How he/she remembers meeting your uncle/aunt

His/Her best memories of courtship

His/Her wedding date, place & his/her funniest memory

Children's names and dates of birth

The rest of the story

Your Aunt or Uncle *Your Father's Sibling*

Full name

Date & place of birth

Birth weight length eye color hair color

Family resemblances

First religious ceremony & attendants

Childhood home(s)

Friends & pets of childhood

Relationships with siblings

Fondest memories

Funniest moments

Special talents & activities

Childhood mischief

Proudest moments

affix photo here if desired

School performance & dreams

Fads, phases & crazes

Education/occupation/military service

How he/she remembers meeting your uncle/aunt

His/Her best memories of courtship

His/Her wedding date, place & his/her funniest memory

Children's names and dates of birth

The rest of the story

Your Grandmother *Your Father's Mother*

Full name

Date & place of birth

Birth weight length eye color hair color

Family resemblances

Brothers' & sisters' names & dates of birth

First religious ceremony & attendants

Childhood home(s)

Friends & pets of childhood

Relationships with siblings

Fondest memories

Funniest moments

Special talents & activities

Childhood mischief

affix photo here if desired

Proudest moments

School performance & dreams

Fads, phases & crazes

Education/occupation

How she remembers meeting your grandfather

Her best memories of courtship

Her wedding date, place & her funniest memory

The rest of the story

Your Great-Grandmother *Your Father's Mother's Mother*

Full name

Date & place of birth

Birth weight length eye color hair color

Family resemblances

Brothers' & sisters' names & dates of birth

First religious ceremony & attendants

Childhood home(s)

Friends & pets of childhood

Relationships with siblings

Fondest memories

Funniest moments

Special talents & activities

Childhood mischief

affix photo here if desired

Proudest moments

School performance & dreams

Fads, phases & crazes

Education/occupation

How she remembers meeting your great-grandfather

Her best memories of courtship

Her wedding date, place & her funniest memory

The rest of the story

Your Great-Grandfather *Your Father's Mother's Father*

Full name

Date & place of birth

Birth weight length eye color hair color

Family resemblances

Brothers' & sisters' names & dates of birth

First religious ceremony & attendants

Childhood home(s)

Friends & pets of childhood

Relationships with siblings

Fondest memories

Funniest moments

Special talents & activities

Childhood mischief

affix photo here if desired

Proudest moments

School performance & dreams

Fads, phases & crazes

Education/occupation/military service

How he remembers meeting your great-grandmother

His best memories of courtship

His wedding date, place & his funniest memory

The rest of the story

Your Grandfather *Your Father's Father*

Full name

Date & place of birth

Birth weight length eye color hair color

Family resemblances

Brothers' & sisters' names & dates of birth

First religious ceremony & attendants

Childhood home(s)

Friends & pets of childhood

Relationships with siblings

Fondest memories

Funniest moments

Special talents & activities

Childhood mischief

affix photo here if desired

Proudest moments

School performance & dreams

Fads, phases & crazes

Education/occupation/military service

How he remembers meeting your grandmother

His best memories of courtship

His wedding date, place & his funniest memory

The rest of the story

Your Great-Grandmother *Your Father's Father's Mother*

Full name

Date & place of birth

Birth weight length eye color hair color

Family resemblances

Brothers' & sisters' names & dates of birth

First religious ceremony & attendants

Childhood home(s)

Friends & pets of childhood

Relationships with siblings

Fondest memories

Funniest moments

Special talents & activities

Childhood mischief

affix photo here if desired

Proudest moments

School performance & dreams

Fads, phases & crazes

Education/occupation

How she remembers meeting your great-grandfather

Her best memories of courtship

Her wedding date, place & her funniest memory

The rest of the story

Your Great-Grandfather *Your Father's Father's Father*

Full name

Date & place of birth

Birth weight length eye color hair color

Family resemblances

Brothers' & sisters' names & dates of birth

First religious ceremony & attendants

Childhood home(s)

Friends & pets of childhood

Relationships with siblings

Fondest memories

Funniest moments

Special talents & activities

Childhood mischief

affix photo here if desired

Proudest moments

School performance & dreams

Fads, phases & crazes

Education/occupation/military service

How he remembers meeting your great-grandmother

His best memories of courtship

His wedding date, place & his funniest memory

The rest of the story

The Rest of the Story

Use this page to record more family stories, affix additional photographs, or to attach an envelope with photocopied pages for extended family members.